:thelwell.
GOES WEST

also by Norman Thelwell

Angels on Horseback
Thelwell Country
Thelwell in Orbit
A Place of Your Own
A Leg at Each Corner
Thelwell's Riding Academy
Top Dog
Up the Garden Path
Compleat Tangler
Thelwell's Book of Leisure
This Desirable Plot
The Effluent Society
Penelope
Thelwell's Magnificat
Three Sheets in the Wind
Belt Up
Thelwell's Pony Cavalcade
Thelwell's Brat Race
Thelwell's Gymkhana
A Plank Bridge by a Pool
A Millstone Round My Neck
Some Damn Fool's Signed the Rubens Again
Thelwell's Sporting Prints
Wrestling with a Pencil
Play It as It Lies
Thelwell's Pony Panorama
Penelope Rides Again
The Cat's Pyjamas

thelwell.
GOES WEST

Mandarin

A Mandarin Humour Paperback

THELWELL GOES WEST

First published in Great Britain in 1975 by Methuen London Ltd
First paperback edition published in 1979
Reissued in 1993 by Mandarin Paperbacks,
an imprint of Reed Consumer Books Ltd
Michelin House, 81 Fulham Road, London SW3 6RB
and Auckland, Melbourne, Singapore and Toronto

Copyright © 1975 by Norman Thelwell

ISBN 0 7493 1083 9
A CIP catalogue record for this book
is available at the British Library

Printed and bound in Great Britain
by Cox & Wyman Ltd, Reading, Berkshire

CONTENTS

The English Rider   6

The Western Horseman   7

Western Riding   9

What to Wear   21

Western Horses   27

Quick on the Drawl   35

How to Understand your Horse   45

On the Trail   57

How to Manage a Mean Horse   73

How to Cross Water   85

Rodeo Dough   91

Western Quiz   101

BULL FINCH

RIDING HABIT

VIEW HALLOO

SADDLE SORE

WHIPPERS IN

HORSE TRAILER

HAY BAG

FOLLOWERS

THRUSTERS

THE ENGLISH RIDER

THE WESTERN
HORSEMAN

WESTERN RIDING

**Before taking up western riding –
it is important to study the cowboy seat**

WESTERN RIDING

In the West, riders find it more comfortable
to sit as low as possible in the saddle –

And to keep one hand free of the reins at all times

Ask them to show you their hands,
when you get a chance and

Notice the relaxed position
adopted by most cowboys when riding the range

– Or when they hit town

The Eastern rider likes to bump up and down in the saddle

This is all very well over short distances but remember –

The cow-hand may be on the trail for weeks at a time

When communicating his wishes to his horse,
the cowboy does so via the animal's neck

Some English methods are not considered good practice

When out on the range --

Your survival may well depend
upon your pony's natural courage –

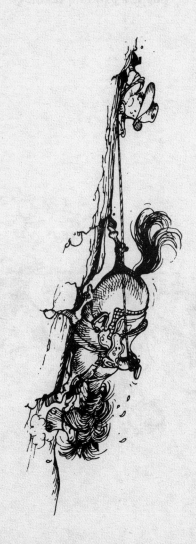

And sure footedness

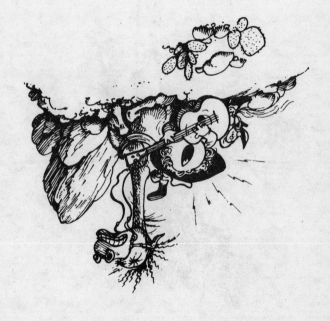

So treat him like a friend

WHAT TO WEAR

The riders of the West are easy-going, outdoor guys and gals
and love to travel light –

They pride themselves
on their simple and practical form of dress

And are inclined to greet fancy clothes with amusement

The saddle is heavier and more complicated than you may
have been used to –

So make sure you know how to put it on correctly

When done by an expert, it all looks very simple

Don't forget to tighten up the cinches

WESTERN HORSES

THE MUSTANG

Known the world over for his unique contribution to the
motion picture industry, this lovable horse has appeared in
more films than Billy-the-Kid

THE QUARTER HORSE

Has great cattle sense and is able
to get off the mark with astonishing speed

THE BRONCO

His name comes from the Spanish word
meaning rough and rude

THE PINTO
or Painted Horse

Natural camouflage gave this animal
a great advantage in battle.
He was much favoured by the Indians
when on the war-path –

So was the APALOOSA or Spotted Horse

THE AMERICAN SADDLE HORSE

Famous for his ability to execute an astonishing variety of
spectacular gaits

THE MORGAN HORSE

This striking little animal has left his imprint on almost every
other American breed

THE PALOMINO

Known as the golden horse of the West,
this handsome creature is popular with all those
who appreciate natural beauty

QUICK ON THE DRAWL

To understand the cowboy's way of life
it is advisable to know the meaning of
certain words and phrases much used by the experts

Here are a few:

Tender Foot (or Hop-a-Long)

Side kicks

The lone stranger

A sod buster or –

Getting yourself a little spread

Speaking with forked tongue

High noon

Getting the drop on a guy

Looking down the barrel of a colt

Get along little dogie

HOW TO UNDERSTAND
YOUR HORSE

Horses cannot talk.
It is useful, therefore, to have some idea
of what they may be thinking

Important clues to your pony's thoughts may be gleaned by close observation of his ears

For example:

'I intend to shoot off to the left'

'You have shot off to the right'

'There's a nasty wind blowing up'.

'Make for cover – It's a twister'

'I am going to gallop under this low tree branch'

'What a dreadful name to call a pony'

The Expert can read his horse from both ends of course

'You want to chase cows – you chase cows'

'You'll never get me up in one of those things'

Notice his general demeanour

You will soon learn what he is trying to say:

'Ooh! Ooh! I've trodden on your guitar'

'It sounded like a rattle-snake to me'

'It's freezing out there on the prairie'

'All this riding off into the sunset is ruining my eyes'

ON THE TRAIL

Before saddling up –
make sure your horse is healthy,
alert and ready to go –

He should be trained to step over
fallen timber without hesitation

And be prepared to carry extra loads
when called upon to do so

He must not spook at harmless objects

Or blunder headlong into dangerous ones

Do not get anxious on difficult terrain – you may communicate your feelings to your horse

And *don't* lean over in the saddle when tired

You may upset his balance

Always dismount on the uphill side of your pony

And if you start an avalanche –
shout a warning to riders below

Be prepared to trust his natural instincts and abilities
when crossing narrow bridges

And do not allow him into water if he is hot

In very hot conditions –
allow him to take advantage of any available shade

And raise his saddle from time to time
to let the air circulate

It is bad manners to ride too close to the horse in front

Or attempt to overtake on a narrow trail

And most important of all

Never ride over private property without
first obtaining the owner's consent

HOW TO MANAGE
A MEAN HORSE

REFUSING TO BE CAUGHT

This can be very trying. Decoy him to some convenient spot
and be ready to slip a rope over his head
without arousing his suspicion

MOVING OFF WHEN ABOUT
TO BE MOUNTED

An exasperating habit. Try the old Indian trick
of leading him into a bog and mounting up
whilst his movement is restricted

BLANKET TEARING

He is probably bored – try singing a different song

VIOLENT PULLING ON THE REINS

This can unseat a rider – have a look at his mouth –
he may have sore teeth

CRIB BITING

The animal should be isolated – the habit is catching

77

WIND SUCKING

Get rid of the horse – the results can be alarming

BITING

Can often be cured – stop carrying sugar lumps
in your back pocket

SUDDEN REARING

The answer here is to slip out of the saddle
whenever he does it

ROLLING

This is natural to a horse and one of his chief joys

Do not let it depress you

BOLTING

Try jerking his head violently backwards and forwards
by pulling on the reins – the idea here
is that it will tend to confuse him

KICKING

**May well be caused by nervousness –
try to comfort and reassure him**

SAVAGING

A frightening sight – drop everything –
run like a jack rabbit

HOW TO CROSS WATER

Do not try to force him into the water against his will

Demonstrate to him that the water is harmless

He will go in when he is ready

Do not dismount and lead him from in front

He is likely to climb on to anything that looks solid.

Make sure you know how to administer the kiss of life –

You never know who may need it

RODEO DOUGH

A great deal of money goes into the rodeo ring these days
so it is as well to study some of the rules

Participants are expected to be reasonably competent before entering the arena

And to perform a pattern of movement
exactly as specified by the judges

Some riders choose to demonstrate their skill in the saddle

Some perform bareback

Others appear to be happier on a bull

Each rider must stay aboard
for a specified number of seconds

And must rake the shoulders
of his mount continuously with his heels

On no account must he touch his horse with his hands

A mild mannered animal may cost him valuable points –

But extra marks may be awarded for style

In case of doubt –

The competitor may be asked to repeat his performance

WESTERN QUIZ

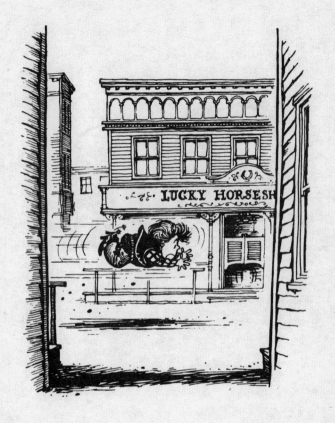

Q. Why is this cowboy shooting up the town?

A. Because his horse stopped suddenly on Main Street

Q. Is this guy a bronco buster?

A. No, but he soon will be if he goes on feeding corn at that rate

Q. Study this picture.
How can you tell that this is a bad man?

A. He has neglected to check his horse's feet for rocks

Q. What is meant by the expression 'Windy Draws'?

A. It is a term of contempt for nervous cowboys

Q. This pony has four weak points – what are they?

A. His legs

Q. Why is this considered bad riding out West?

A. The head should be up and the heels down

Q. Is this cowpoke being chased by a posse?

A. No. The correct name is Cougar or Mountain Lion

Q. Why is this rider looking uncomfortable?

A. His jeans are too tight

Q. Would you call this guy a saddle tramp?

A. If it was your saddle you would

Q. What is wrong with this picture?

A. The rider has got the wrong foot in the stirrup

Q. What important rule did this rider neglect?

A. She did not check the brand before buying her pony

And finally –
What is the most important rule to remember?

That's right! *Never* hold onto the reins with both hands